Marriage Ain't for Punks

Written by Shar'ron Mason

Marriage Ain't for Punks
Copyright © 2017 by Shar'ron Mason

All rights reserved. No part of this book may be reproduced or transmitted in any form or by any means without written permission from the author.

ISBN: 0-692-93254-2
ISBN-13: 978-0-692-93254-4

Dedication

The fact that you are reading this book is a true testament to God's goodness and faithfulness. Without Him I would have given up on this book a long time ago and embarked on yet another journey. I thank God for His constant reminders to me of the purpose of this book, 'To change lives.' Thank you Lord for letting me know that I was never alone and that this book is a part of your Great Plan for my life.

I've often heard it said, "Behind every good man is a good woman." This may often be the case, but what I have personally experienced is a great man standing behind and beside me along my journey. To that man; my husband, my honey, my king, Darrell, thanks for your encouragement, support and especially the example that you've set.

I'd also like to thank my parents for their unconditional love. Mama, your prophetic words and encouragement have been priceless. Your words haven't fallen on deaf ears. Daddy, your giving spirit is admirable. I strive to display it a little more each day.

To my daughter, Breonna, I pray that God continues to reveal His desires for your journey and that love, joy and peace are your constant companions each step that you take.

To my editor, Ashley, thanks for your help in bringing *Marriage Ain't for Punks* to life. I appreciate the time that you committed to my project.

To my accountability partner and sounding board, La Tonya, thank you for your countless hours of support and embracing my project as your own. Your pushing and pulling in the home stretch made a huge difference.

To my family and friends who have prayed for me and encouraged me along the way, "Thank you!"

Table of Contents

Pages

Preface 7
Introduction 10
Who is This Book For? 13
How Can You Use This Book? 16

Punks...

Marry for All the Wrong Reasons 18
Don't Want to Work 23
Send Their Representative 27
Continue to Act Single After Saying
   "I Do" 32
Exploit Vulnerabilities 36
Walk into Marriage with an Out in
   Mind 40
Think They Know-It-All 44
Run When Things Get Tough 49
Seek Solutions in All the Wrong
   Places 53
Refuse to Adjust Unrealistic
   Expectations 57
Make Excuses Instead of Making
   Changes 61
Don't Take the Time to Get to Know
   Themselves 65
Are Stuck in the Past 68

Are Controlling.................	71
Can't Hold Water	74
Fail to Leave and Cleave	78
Refuse to Say "I'm Sorry"	82
Are Pushovers..................	85
Have No Sense of Humor	89
Stop Studying Their Spouse	93
Expect Perfection	97
I'm Still Not Sold on This Punk Thing	101
Inventory	103
You are Undeniably a Punk. Now What?...................	107

Preface

When I tell people the title of my book, I often get an inquisitive look. '*Marriage Ain't for Punks*, hmmm... What's that all about?' In fact, the title may be the reason that you picked up this book. So, what's the big deal? What's this punk thing all about? To be successfully married requires a special skill-set; the willingness and ability to acknowledge and address one's own mess. A punk is a person who refuses to address their relationship-repellent attitudes, behaviors and characteristics; thereby making it impossible to have a healthy marriage.

That's a mouthful, but the concept is rather simple. If you are a punk, you can not have a happy, healthy marriage. Either you will be miserable or your mate will; in fact, there's a chance you'll both be miserable. Who walks into marriage saying, 'I want to be miserable?' No one does; however, that's what the punk has to look forward to if he or she doesn't make some internal changes.

I won't lie to you. The transformation process is difficult. Change isn't easy and it's far easier to place the blame on someone else than it is to accept responsibility for who you are *today*. We've all been negatively affected by the actions and choices of others, but at some point we must decide, with the help of God, to create the life we want.

If you're the person who would rather point the finger at the next person and blame them for your failed relationship, this book **isn't** for you. This book is for the person who wants to purge the punk from the inside out and truly have a chance at a great marriage.

Aside from change being difficult, another reason that many people don't change is that few people *truly* want to change. Comfort doesn't precede change, discomfort does. So, if you are comfortable with who you are, the good and the bad, there is a great chance that you won't take this process serious. If your motto is, "this is who I am" or you believe you can't change, then you won't embark on the journey of transformation.

We all bring our fair share of baggage to a relationship, but I hope this book serves as a vessel to help minimize that baggage and empower you to overcome and withstand the challenges that inevitably come, simply by being human.

We must be intentional about working on *ourselves* or risk the very relationships that we prayed and sometimes begged for. I pray that you are able to benefit from the experiences shared in this book. When you see yourself in these pages, don't lose heart. God can transform you. Acknowledge your shortcomings and put forth the effort necessary to change. The wonderful marriage that you desire is closer than you think.

Introduction

It never ceases to amaze me when I encounter a newly married couple that has only been married a matter of months, who are already spewing the dreaded "D" word at one another. "I'm tired of your mess. I want a divorce." "I don't have to take this. I'm done. I'm filing for a divorce." "I have needs and you're not fulfilling them. I'll see you in court."

I just want to grab them by the shoulders, shake them hard and yell in their faces, "What did you think you were signing up for, punk? Put on your overalls and lace your boot straps up tight. It's time to work!" But as a marriage therapist, relationship coach and law abiding citizen, I know it's not acceptable to grab people, shake them or yell at them, so I don't, but believe me the thought often goes through my mind. Then I also have to remember that I was once in those same shoes. *Ouch*, the truth *does* hurt sometimes.

We've all heard that there's no "I" in team, but the bottom line is, many people don't sign up to be on a team when they marry. They sign up to get what they want. And when "I" don't feel happy, satisfied, fulfilled, comforted, supported, loved, respected, heard, understood, wanted, etc…, "I" start looking for ways to change how "I" feel. I have yet to hear someone say, "I want a divorce because I'm not meeting her needs" or "I'm leaving him because I don't make him happy." I'm sure *someone* has spoken those words, but I have never heard them.

Too many people get married who have no business getting married. They are punks. That is the real reason behind so many marriages ending in divorce. They say they want to be married, but they are punks who refuse to work on their relationship-repellent attitudes, behaviors and characteristics. These attitudes, behaviors and characteristics may have been acceptable or served them "well" as a single person but they are detrimental to a healthy marriage.

I'm sure you can name someone who fits my description of a punk. Guess what? *You* may be that person who comes to mind when others think of a punk with relationship-repellent tendencies. I pray that this book will help you to see yourself more clearly and I encourage you to honestly evaluate yourself as you move through these pages. Ask yourself, "Do I fit the bill of the punk being described?" Brace yourself for the truth and more importantly prepare for what is to come. God can and will transform you, if you give Him room to move and come along as a partner on your journey. Are you ready? Let's go!

Who is This Book For?

Are you single? Are you married? Are you divorced? Are you engaged? Are you in a "committed" relationship? *Marriage Ain't for Punks* is for you, you, you, you and you. No, really! This book is for each of you.

For the single person who desires to marry someday, this is the perfect time to look at your relationship-repellent attitudes, behaviors and characteristics that may be the demise of your future marriage if not addressed. It can be more difficult to look at yourself when you're in a relationship with another flawed individual. The tendency is to point the finger and focus on what they need to fix and to minimize your mess. So, single person, this book is for you.

The divorce rate continues to be staggering and the number of couples who miserably co-exist or drudge along is just as sobering. If you're the married punk who refuses to deal with your relationship-repellent attitudes, behaviors and characteristics chances are you'll someday join the ranks of the divorced or the miserably drudging along. So, yes this book is for you. The challenge for the married and the divorced will be to take your focus off of your spouse's (ex-spouse's) flaws and take a good look at yourself. By addressing your mess you are setting yourself up for a successful marriage now or for a marriage that doesn't follow in the footsteps of your failed marriage. So, married folks, divorced folks, *Marriage Ain't for Punks* IS for you.

Are you thinking about jumping the broom, getting hitched, tying the knot? Well, regardless of what terms you use to describe making the marital commitment, this book is for you. In working with pre-marital couples, whether through pre-marital counseling or pre-marital workshops or groups, I've found that many couples have a plan to marry and that's the focus. Some are just going through the motions with the counseling and groups to check them off the marriage preparation list; however, they don't want to look at the warning signs and glaring red lights before them. If you are that person, *Marriage Ain't for Punks* ISN'T for you. If you want to deal with your internal punk prior to marriage and give your marriage a chance at a long healthy life this book IS for you.

I would also highly suggest you take an inventory of your beloved's mess while you're taking your own. This is the time to seriously consider if you can accept what your man/woman is bringing to the table. Many times mates think that they can change one another. Yes, people change, but just know that you should not say "I Do" based on your belief that your man will change or your woman will get her act together. If you can't accept him with his flaws today, then you shouldn't be headed to the altar. Ok, I'll step off my soapbox for a minute, but in all sincerity, save yourself the frustration and headache.

 I'm a Christian. It shows in my walk and in my talk. It's a part of every fiber of my being. It's actually the part of me that I'm most proud of. Yes, this book is for my fellow Christians for sure. But, this book has rich morsels for the non-Christian as well. The only requirement for the reader is a desire to gain greater insight into some of the relationship-repellent attitudes, behaviors and characteristics that make it next to impossible to have a healthy marriage. And if you want to go a step further to deal with your mess, *Marriage Ain't for Punks* can help you with that as well.

How Can You Use This Book?

There are many ways that you can use this book. *Marriage Ain't for Punks* can be used as an accompaniment to your therapeutic work. You can go solo and read this book by yourself. You can read this book with others who know you well. Or you can read *Marriage Ain't for Punks* in a discussion group format.

As a Marriage and Family Therapist, it feels great to work with a client who is fully engaged in their healing/transformation process. This book can be used to bring greater insight into the relationship-repellent attitudes, behaviors and characteristics that are making it difficult to obtain and maintain healthy relationships overall and more specifically the marital relationship. The client and therapist can use *Marriage Ain't for Punks* to discover more about underlying issues and dis-ease that are plaguing the client. Yes, as a therapist I am partial, but I know that this book can foster the healing process and positively impact therapeutic work.

You can read *Marriage Ain't for Punks* by yourself and take note of the times that you see yourself in what you're reading. If you're self-aware or pretty insightful, this may work very well. In addition, in reading alone, you can use this book as a guide in looking at what your future mate brings to the table or in having constructive conversation with your current mate.

This book can also be read with others who know you well, such as your spouse/significant other, good friend, or accountability partner. This gives you the benefit of receiving feedback on the relationship-repellent attitudes, behaviors and characteristics that may be blind spots for you.

One more way that *Marriage Ain't for Punks* can be read is in a group format of sorts. This could be a small cell group or book club. This will allow you to discuss the aspects of being a punk in more detail with others who also desire to nip punkship in the bud in hopes of an amazing marriage now or in the future.

I'm sure there are other ways that this book can be used also and hey, you've bought it, so feel free to use it however it'll best meet your needs. Feel free to drop me a line at lovethatrelationship@gmail.com to tell me about the ways that you've used *Marriage Ain't for Punks* for your benefit.

Punks Marry for All the Wrong Reasons

 Gerald is what women call: fine, built, a stud. At least that's what Debra thought when she first noticed him in the conference room at her job. Debra soon learned that Gerald was a consultant with his own law firm. Debra had just broken up with her boyfriend after catching him kissing a "colleague" and knew that her ex would go crazy if he saw Debra with Gerald. HANDSOME, INTELLIGENT and SUCCESSFUL. Yes! Gerald was the one.

 So, Debra made it her mission to get with Gerald. She wanted her ex to hurt. She wanted him to pay. She wanted her ex to burn with jealousy. Debra pursued Gerald hard from that first day. With her inside "connections" she just so happened to always be in the right place at the right time. She made sure she dressed the part, walked the part and talked the part.

 Debra's plan worked. Soon, she and Gerald were an item. And it didn't take long for Debra and Gerald to "accidentally" run into her ex at the mall. Debra thought, 'See, it didn't take long for me to move on and forget about you. How do you feel now?'

But, the truth is that Debra still had deep feelings for her ex. Gerald was the "perfect" man, but even in his "perfection" he couldn't heal her broken heart.

The little game didn't stop with infuriating her ex. Debra loved the way that other women would look at her with envy when she and Gerald were together. Her friends and family would often comment on how great they looked together and how they made the "perfect" couple. Debra enjoyed being complimented on her good "catch." And once Debra learned that Gerald's family had money it was settled. She decided to keep Gerald around.

FAST FORWARD 5 YEARS

Debra and Gerald have been married for 3 ½ years, but they have very little in common. Their sex life was explosive in the beginning, but even it has fizzled. Gerald once enjoyed being shown off by Debra, but that's played out too. He's grown tired of being Debra's trophy and even more so of having a shallow relationship. He loves Debra, but he knows that the feeling is not mutual. He thought, eventually, that would change.

Gerald has never minded showering Debra with expensive gifts and exotic trips, but that seems to be all she wants from him these days. Gerald can still see the slight smirk on Debra's lips when they ran into her ex in the mall what seems like ages ago. As intelligent as Gerald is, it has taken him this long to realize that that was no "coincidence."

Debra is a Punk that married for all the wrong reasons!

Hot sex, long money, big house, a banging body; if these are among the shallow reasons that you entered into marriage; you're in for a rude awakening. All of these things can be gone quickly and then what? Are you going to leave and pursue these things with someone else? Punk, you're asking for trouble when you say "I do" simply because she cooks a mean T-bone.

So many marriages start on the wrong premise that it's no wonder so many end in divorce. How many ways can you hang from the chandelier and please her physically? I know you're trying to find out, but that can't be the long-term glue for your marriage.

We all know what the love of money is...the root of all evil (1 Timothy 6:10). And it can buy a lot of material goods, but it truly can't buy happiness. Look at all of the rich folks losing their minds and killing themselves, by various means. They have a boatload of money, but they're miserable. Material possessions can make life more comfortable, but they require more responsibility and work to keep them. And looks. Well, you can staple, nip, tuck, inject, and exercise to your hearts content, but those looks will eventually go south like your chin and your gluteus maximus.

What is your reason for marrying? Are you trying to escape your current situation? Bad reason. Are you just looking for someone to take care of you or your children? Wrong motive. Partnership? Mutual support? To fulfill God's plan for your life? Good reasons. Good motives. A good marriage requires a solid foundation to stand on, something that can anchor you when times get tough. Don't build your marriage on quick sand. It won't stand.

Decide to create a marriage that brings glory to God. Walk into marriage realizing that many things can and will change in the course of your marriage. A common vision and commitment to something bigger than your spouse and your self will be paramount every step of the way. A mutually satisfying marriage is a good reason to give it all you've got.

Punks Don't Want to Work

Maggie thought it was admirable for Mike to suggest that he stay home with their infant son after Maggie's maternity leave ended. That would give Mike and Junior an opportunity to bond and besides childcare for Junior would be a whopping $275 per week. The first couple of months, everything seemed fine with Mike and Junior, but Maggie soon realized that all was not what it seemed.

One day, Maggie came home on her lunch hour to change into a more comfortable pair of shoes. Mike was asleep on the couch, but Junior was nowhere to be found. Maggie shook Mike to wake him and he looked shocked to see her standing over him. Mike told Maggie that Junior was at his mom's house for a little while. Maggie felt that there was more to the story and when she asked Mike how long this, "taking Junior to your mom's thing" had been going on, Mike became defensive. He said, "I'm a grown man and I don't appreciate you checking up on me. You know it's hard for me to write when there's stuff going on around me. And besides, my mama loves watching Junior." Maggie reminded Mike that they agreed that he would work while pursuing his passion for writing. Mike said, "I don't know why you're sweating me about a job. You make more than enough to handle our bills."

Maggie told Mike that she needed to get back to work, but she wanted to discuss this situation when she got off work. Maggie can't believe she fell for the okey doke. She should have known there was more to Mike wanting to stay home and bond with Junior. Mike did his fair share of feeding and attending to Junior, but he was definitely not a fan of #2 diapers.

Mike is a Punk that doesn't want to work!

It's a four letter word, W.O. R. K. For most people it isn't offensive, but for the punk who doesn't want to work, it's a fighting word. This punk will think of every excuse under the sun not to work; the economy is bad, they won't hire me, my back is bad, I can't get to work, I don't have enough experience, I don't have enough education, I'm still trying to find myself, and on and on and on. Just face it, punk, you don't want to work. You want someone else to take care of your needs and your wants. You may even think it's their responsibility or that the world owes you something. If both partners have sat down and discussed this arrangement, that's one thing, but if you, like Mike, just decided that your man or your woman will take care of you, that's another story.

This punk may be well educated with degrees, but still have no intentions of using them; a lifetime student. Lazy? Now that's debatable because this punk is probably pretty active in all other ways, but mention J. O.B. and you may as well have called him or her an S.O.B. because here comes the fight. "I'm still trying to figure out what I want to do." "I'd support you if the shoe was on the other foot." "When I get paid, you'll be well taken care of."

You may be the punk that is always coming up with some get rich quick scheme. They don't take any work, but they're going to net you big bucks. If it sounds too good to be true, it probably is, so stop wasting your time trying to figure out how to get rich without putting forth any effort. If you're not willing to work to bring your ideas to fruition they'll never become a reality, not for you anyway. The great business ventures in your mind may be promising for tomorrow, but you need to bring some legitimate funds into your household today.

Don't you realize that you can work on those ideas while you work to support yourself? It's wise to work to have money for your immediate needs; food, housing and clothing, while working on your business idea. And don't even think about giving your mate the guilt trip to support you for the next 20 years. The Bible says in 2 Thessalonians 3:10, that the man that doesn't work doesn't eat. Maybe it's time you start missing a few meals. I'm sure you'll have a new found appreciation for work then.

Punks Send Their Representative

Rona and Stan met at a cooking class at a local college in their community. They clicked during the second class when they were paired together. Stan loved Rona's independent spirit. Rona had an air of confidence and carried herself well. She seemed proud of raising her son and daughter alone after her husband abandoned their family and had no problem sharing her impressive plans to open a bed and breakfast in the near future.

During their courtship, Rona and Stan talked about all aspects of their lives. They shared their hopes and dreams as well as their past failures. Stan often thought, 'how can I be so blessed to have found a woman so genuine and loving?' Stan felt as if he'd known Rona his entire life.
FAST FORWARD 4 YEARS
Stan and Rona have only been married 3 months, but Stan is already realizing that the woman he met in that cooking class and spent countless hours in conversation with and the woman that he is married to are not the same person. How could Rona make up blatant lies regarding her own children? It now makes sense why Rona's children spent

so much time at her parents' home. Rona's parents are her children's guardians. Rona could no longer hide the truth after Stan came across the guardianship papers in Rona's briefcase. Rona's explanation for her children staying at her parents' home to remain at the "good" school in her parent's district made pretty good sense to Stan when they discussed it initially. After all, who doesn't want their children to get a stellar education? But, it made no sense once Stan and Rona moved into their new home in a district equally as impressive.

The deception doesn't end there. It seems that Rona's "independence" had been made possible through the monthly "allowance" her parents consistently deposited into her account each month. Stan soon put two and two together. This was a condition of the "agreement" allowing Rona's parents to retain custody of her children trouble free. Rona's parents only gave her what she asked for to save their grandchildren more unnecessary pain in court. This discovery totally infuriated Stan. He would never dream of mistreating his parents in any way. Stan's parents are financially stable, but he still insists on paying for a vacation for them once a year.

He says that's the least he can do for the many sacrifices that they made for him and his siblings over the years. Stan can't understand what would possess Rona to use her parents.

And where did the confident Rona disappear to? Stan can't affirm Rona enough these days. Rona needs constant attention and assurance. She has to be under Stan 24/7 and orchestrates elaborate schemes in an attempt to spend more time with him. Stan is a patient man, but he's about at his wits end with Rona. How could Stan have been so naïve? It's easier than you think when dealing with a person who sends their representative. Poor Stan was a victim of the big switcheroo.

Rona is a Punk who sent her representative!

Now, I'm not talking about waking up on your honeymoon to a person with a different eye color, hair length, and/or body dimensions than when you walked down the aisle. Many people turn it up a notch on their "big day." Punk, you know if you sent your representative to close the deal. The representative was nice, polite, respectful, attentive and giving. Now the real you is an evil, vindictive, stingy, lying, cheater. You knew you were putting on an act. You knew that the person your mate was falling for was not truly *you*. Instead of doing what it took to become that ideal mate, you decided to pretend to be someone that you were not.

You're one of the worst types of punks because you come fully in disguise and sweep innocent victims off their feet. You make it difficult for them to trust again. You're ruining lives and thinking nothing of it.

Does your representative have great credit, but the real you has a negative credit score? Does your representative love children, but you despise them? Is your representative a philanthropist, but you're truly a gold digger? Your mind is diabolical and you may or may not even be aware of the game that you're playing. No marriage can be healthy when the parties involved send their reps.

How long do you think you can keep on your mask? Just until you say, "I do"? If the real you is a womanizer or a man-hater, it's going to be revealed. If the real you is a liar, a dope fiend, a pimp, a drama queen, jealous, etc…it's going to be revealed, so you might as well put it out there and let your love interest make an informed decision. "He wouldn't accept me if he knew..." Well, probably not, but he deserves to know. "She wouldn't like me if she saw this part of me." Maybe she would or maybe she wouldn't, but, punk, give her an opportunity to decide for herself.

You will feel so much better about yourself and your relationship when you take off the mask. Become the person that you're trying to portray. There is no way around it. Do the work!

Punks Continue to Act Single After Saying "I Do"

"Give me 20 minutes to throw on some clothes and I'll meet you there. I heard the new band is hot." Russell can't believe his ears. Once again his wife, Marie, is bailing out on their plans so she can go hang with her girls. This will be the third time this week that she's gone out and it's only Thursday.

Russell's thinking to himself, "Marie didn't even hang out this much when she was single." He doesn't want to argue with Marie, but he can't hold it in. "Marie, I overhead you say that you would meet somebody in a few minutes. Did you forget about our plans?" "Well, my girl Tia is in town and I figured you'd understand. I haven't seen her in a couple months." "Well I don't understand because this is something you do regularly. You act like you're still single. I don't expect you to ask permission to hang out, but I would appreciate some common courtesy and consideration." "There you go again, trying to control me. Stop tripping and trying to change me."

Marie and her girls have been hanging out and clubbing since college. She has no intentions of changing that now. Sure, she plans to slow down at some point, but right now she's having a ball. Besides, she's still young. She often says that Russell is trying to turn her into his boring mama. Russell enjoys going out too, but the difference is that he puts his time with Marie first and makes sure they don't already have plans before he makes plans with other folks.

Marie is a Punk that still acts single after saying, "I do"

What has changed in your life since saying "I do"? You don't take your spouse into consideration when you make decisions. You still go where you want to go, when you want to go and with whom you want to go. You participated in a ceremony to join two lives, but not much has changed. You still have a single's mentality and from the looks of it you have no intentions of changing that. You seem to want the benefits of marriage with the perks of singlehood. That may work pretty well for you punk, but what about your spouse? If you both have the same mentality, you may be able to operate in this way, but if not, they're getting the short end of the stick.

    This can translate in several ways, you may be like roommates sharing financial responsibilities, but be emotionally and intimately distant. You may be like casual lovers sharing a bed with no other ties binding you. You may be single outside of your home, but married when you walk through your doors. The scenarios are many and I'm sure you understand what I'm saying. You're single in ways that benefit you and married in other ways that benefit you. A single person is able to make decisions without consulting anyone. They can come and go as they please. If you said, "I do" that single person is no longer *you*.

    Punk, when you said "I do" you became a part of something called a marriage. Marriage is about being a unit. It is about mutuality. Mutual benefits, mutual respect, mutual commitment, and mutual sacrifice for something bigger than either of you. You have to constantly consider how your decisions will affect your relationship and your spouse, not just how it will affect you. You must focus not only on the pleasure and comfort a decision will bring you, but how that decision will impact your mate.

Marriage affects every part of your life. It's not about you anymore. Give that some serious thought. It's about "we" and "us" now. Your single friends probably won't appreciate the new you or understand why you can't just "do you" anymore. That's ok, because one day that great transformation will probably take place in their lives too. When they go from singlehood to coupledom, they'll need to change and embrace this new mindset too. Be a good example of what that looks like. Being married is not about begrudgingly losing yourself. When you and your mate yield to God in a marriage covenant, you'll become a better you than you ever imagined.

Punks Exploit Vulnerabilities

Chelsie had a rough childhood. Her father was very abusive to her and her mother. Chelsie can remember her father leaving to visit a "relative" out of town when she was about 8 years old and never returning. Although Chelsie never endured her father's physical abuse again, she often felt sad because her mother's entire demeanor changed after her father left. Her once vivacious loving mother was now solemn and withdrawn. Chelsie always felt responsible for her father's leaving and consequently felt guilty for her mother's condition.

Chelsie didn't share her inner struggles of guilt and abandonment with anyone for a long time. She didn't want to appear weak or risk being hurt. She put up a wall and stayed closed off from intimate relationships. Superficial relationships were okay to Chelsie. She didn't need any more than that. But, then she met Roy. Chelsie felt that Roy was different. They could talk for hours about any and everything. Although they seemed like complete opposites, they had an appreciation for one another's aspirations and dreams. Chelsie's wall was quickly crumbling and she was surprised at how at ease she felt with Roy.

One day, about 9 months into their relationship, Chelsie felt safe enough to share the abuse that she had experienced and witnessed with Roy. She told Roy about her feelings of abandonment and even shared how she felt guilty for her father's leaving.

Roy reassured Chelsie that she was not at fault and told her that her father had missed out on knowing a beautiful young woman. Chelsie took a chance and everything was fine. Well, fine until Roy and Chelsie had their first major disagreement. The conversation started out as a simple difference of opinion, but somehow got very heated. Roy stormed out of Chelsie's apartment and didn't call or return Chelsie's calls for 2 weeks. When he did return, he told Chelsie that he could see why her father had left and never came back. Chelsie broke down crying and apologized to Roy feverishly for running him off. Deep down, Roy knew that Chelsie needed to seek help for her issues, but he chose to use them to get what he wanted. Anytime Roy felt threatened or upset because things with

Chelsie weren't going as Roy had planned, he'd quickly turn the tables by throwing Chelsie's weaknesses in her face.

Roy is a Punk that exploits vulnerabilities!

Her father left her when she was a child, so she fears being alone. He was told that he would never amount to anything, so he craves affirmation. She was sexually assaulted, so she fears being taken advantage of. Whatever the vulnerability may be; weight, intelligence, failure; it wasn't shared with you to later be used against your mate. It was shared to provide some insight of how to support and uplift him/her. Punk, why do you take that information and use it for your benefit? Why do you use it as leverage and break your spouse down with it.

Marriage requires vulnerability. This person sees you at your worst, day in and day out, and still accepts you, morning breath and all. You are in a unique place to see and hear things that no one else will. You know what keeps your spouse awake at night and what wakes him/her from their sleep. That is valuable information that should be treated with care. It's precious.

Don't toss it around like a water balloon. And definitely don't throw it in his/her face when you're mad or use it to get your needs met.

You have vulnerabilities too. How would you like your deepest fears and secrets exposed, used against you? It's a scary thought. But marriage is about taking a chance. Placing your best and worst in someone's hands, trusting that they will keep it safe and only use that precious information to help, not harm you, takes faith and trust. From the inside looking out, you have a unique perspective to benefit the relationship. Don't abuse your position. Don't defy your mate's trust and further damage them. If you become a safe haven for your mate, he/she will open up and really share who they are and what has been instrumental to them becoming that person. You are privileged to be in that position. Remember: to whom much is given, much is required. (Luke 12:48)

Punks Walk Into Marriage with an Out in Mind

Ryan has always had a Plan B. His back up plans have always served him well and the million scenarios running through his head have helped him to stay at the top of his game and usually ahead of the pack, but this mindset is becoming lethal to his marriage.

Ryan loves Jacqueline, but he's always thinking in the back of his mind that their marriage won't work out. If you ask him why he feels this way, he'll probably deny that he does feel this way. His words say that he's in this marriage for the long run, but his actions say that he has one foot out the door. Ryan has money put away in an account that Jacqueline isn't aware of and he never gives 100% of himself. Ryan often sits back and replays Jacqueline's every action and their conversations looking for something that isn't right. He has yet to find anything substantial, but he thinks it's only a matter of time.

Jacqueline thinks Ryan is focusing on his career and that's the reason that after 5 years, he's still not ready for children. The reality is that Ryan is just waiting for the other shoe to drop and he doesn't want any extra inconveniences to deal with during their divorce. Ryan has recently begun to look through Jacqueline's phone and checking her odometer. Although Jacqueline has never given him reason to doubt her faithfulness and commitment to their marriage, he keeps thinking that he's bound to find something.

Ryan's friends are all either divorced or they've never been married. They make sly remarks to Ryan saying that he'd better enjoy his marriage while it lasts and 'nothing lasts forever'. Ryan says their comments go in one ear and out the other and although he doesn't say it, he believes the same thing.

Ryan is a Punk who walked into marriage with an out in mind!

We've all seen them and some of us have been them. That couple that we know who won't see their one year anniversary because one or both of them has a laundry list of things that can't/won't be tolerated. "His family better not stop over uninvited." "She better not hang with her old girlfriends." "He better not…" "She better not…" This punk's suitcase is never far away because at any time they may need to pick up and move on.

Do you have a list of things that your mate must or must not do? Have you ever heard the term "self-fulfilling prophesy"? It means what you focus on is most likely what you will get. If you believe your marriage will be a failure, then it probably will be a failure. When you enter marriage with an out in mind, you fail to give your marriage 100%. It's impossible because you're reserving energy for the "great escape". You're constantly on the look-out for the words and actions that can justify you leaving and saying, "I knew it". You probably have a secret stash put aside for this occasion that you call your "rainy day fund".

You're half in the marriage and halfway out; mentally, physically and emotionally. You don't realize it, but fear is robbing you of something great: intimacy. What are you afraid of? Is it losing yourself or being hurt? If you're the punk that I'm describing you need to take some time for introspection. Examine yourself and discover what is causing you to be half in and half out of your relationship. The Bible says that a double-minded man is unstable in all his ways (James 1:8) Give your marriage a fair chance of succeeding by deciding that come hell or high water, you're going to fight for your marriage!

Punks Think They Know-It-All

Bailey is definitely married to a know-it-all. Dean is pretty intelligent which is half the problem itself. The other half of the problem is Dean feels that he has to prove that he knows it all. Let him tell it, he has done everything. Whether it's driving, home improvement projects, or cooking; whatever it is, Dean has the experience, the answer and he can do it better than anyone else. And for the things that Dean has not done, he falls back on other peoples' experience as if it was his own.

Dean often sits back and directs Bailey on how to be a better mother, shopper, gardener and he even gives her pointers on her job as a sales rep. When they watch television, which is rare because Bailey can't take it, Dean re-writes the script, talking through the show about how unrealistic it is or what would make more sense.

Bailey has stopped inviting guests over to their home. A fun evening of dinner and games always ends with Dean monopolizing the conversation "proving" that he knows it all. The guests leave tired and Bailey feels embarrassed. Dean says he doesn't know what the problem is. He can't help that he's had so many experiences and undertaken extensive studies in so many areas. Dean, the problem is that your social skills stink. Your wife doesn't want to spend time with you and she has genuine love for you. Any one who is not required to be in your presence will avoid you at all costs.

Dean is a Punk that thinks he knows it all!

    I worked with a guy once that knew everything. It didn't matter what subject you were discussing, he was an expert. He had worked in every occupation practically and didn't mind letting you know that he had the answer to whatever question you might pose. Yes, he was a know-it-all. It's one thing to work with a know-it-all, you can go to your office or cubicle and just tune him or her out. It's another thing to be married to Mr. or Mrs. Know-It-All. Every conversation becomes like the final round of Jeopardy.
    Know-It-All, it's impressive the amount of knowledge you have, but it's ok to hold a little back. After a while talking to you feels like a competition. Like you're trying to one-up the person you're talking to.

Did you know that sometimes your spouse just wants to be listened to without receiving a response? I know it sounds strange, but it's ok to not have *all* the answers. It's ok to take information in and not let information out. You don't have to build yourself up with a ton of knowledge and facts. You're already important. No one wants to talk to a know-it-all every day. It simply wears you out. Sometimes you just want to have a normal conversation that goes nowhere.

But hey, there are other know-it-alls in the world just like you. Take some time and seek them out. That way you'll have an outlet to discuss the endless knowledge in your head to give your mate a chance to breathe. But then again, know-it-alls really don't want to know what anyone else knows, so that may not be such a good idea. Maybe a journal will serve as a good outlet. Whatever the case, don't be a know-it-all with your man/woman. They may love you to pieces, but they don't always want to hear your vast knowledge about everything under the sun.

There is a saying, "There's more than one way to skin a cat." This punk doesn't believe that. If you don't do it the way he/she does it then you're definitely not doing it the right way. Pick a category, any area and they're an expert: cooking, driving, parenting, shopping, you name it, they have all the answers and don't mind telling you why and how you're doing it wrong. If you're driving, you should have turned that way. If you're shopping she/he would have found a better deal. If you're cleaning, well you get the point.

    I have a news flash for you: you DON'T know everything and your way ISN'T the only way to do things. Punk, you're anal and you need to take a chill pill. What difference does it make how the dishes are stacked, how the laundry is folded, if the grass is cut vertically or horizontally? You're not leaving room for anyone else to contribute and eventually you're going to push them totally out the way. Is being right and knowing everything about everything more important than having a good relationship? If so, keep demanding that things be done to your specifications and you won't have to worry about it because you'll be left alone to do it.

    If you're always right and everyone else is always wrong, how do you think that makes them feel? It doesn't take a rocket scientist to figure it out, not good! Loosen up. Give people a chance to be themselves instead of requiring that they become little clones of you. Stop getting your worth from the little things that you do ever so "perfectly." Go get some help if you can't manage your perfectionism. And if nothing else don't hold others to your unachievable standards.

Punks Run When Things Get Tough

Samantha and George have only been married 15 months and Samantha has already moved out twice. She has had thoughts of leaving at least 3 other times. Their marriage has had a rocky start with George losing his job 2 months after they married and Samantha miscarrying their first child 6 months later, but this pattern of running is not new to Samantha. Whenever things get tough or don't turn out the way that Samantha had hoped, she thinks that it must not be God's will and she moves on to something else.

Samantha has left several great jobs because truth be told, they became too challenging. She has switched churches over minor disagreements, and she even abandoned her dream of becoming an events planner when things didn't just fall in her lap. George and Samantha's mother tried to explain to her that launching anything new is a process and it would work out if she continued to work at it, but Samantha gave up and resigned to stick it out at her current job. She can do her job with her eyes closed and she is often bored out of her mind, but it's something that she knows, so she's still there.

George is hesitant to discuss weighty issues with Samantha because he knows that she is prone to check out mentally, if not physically, when there are tough issues at hand. George has suggested that they talk to their pastor, but Samantha says she's fine, and just not willing to deal with a bunch of nonsense.

Samantha is a Punk that runs when things get tough!

I've been called a quitter a time or two. I didn't want to accept that title at the time, but when I thought about it, I realized that word described me to the T. I made all kinds of excuses, but I couldn't deny the pattern that was behind me. I never wanted to be known as a quitter so I decided to begin finishing things that I started, this book being one of those things.

Do you run when things get tough? If so, good luck in maintaining a marriage or relationship of any sort for that matter. Marriage happens to be one of those things that comes with plenty of tough situations; health issues, financial troubles, communication breakdowns, kid chaos, unrealistic expectations, throw in some in-law or baby mama/daddy drama and you've got a real live marriage staring you in the face.

Has anyone in your life ever cared enough about you to be honest, like people who love me have been? Or do you know yourself well enough to know that you run when things get tough? Don't punk out when it starts looking tough, dig your heals in deep and start working on whatever it is that you can do to make the situation better. Pray and ask God to handle the rest, whether it entails fixing a situation that's out of your control, changing your spouse or transforming stubborn you.

Learning to not give up quickly is important in marriage; however, that doesn't mean that you become someone's punching bag or allow your children to be abused. Come on now, use common sense. I'm talking about situations that don't warrant you running but, calls for work. The past is a good indicator of the future so don't be naïve and think that you'll miraculously become someone who stays put when you've always run in the past. Set your intentions on sustaining and maintaining and you'll be better equipped to endure the rough times.

Punks Seek Solutions in All the Wrong Places

Ron is really mad, and for good reason. He presented an idea to his supervisor and his supervisor presented it to the higher ups as if it was his own. His supervisor will probably get a promotion since the idea is sure to bring hefty dividends into the company. And what will Ron get? NOTHING!

But rather than addressing the issue with his supervisor, Ron is at the bar working on his 6th shot. He and his fiancé, April, have dinner plans, but "she'll just have to understand." Besides, Ron is waiting on his buddy Jerome so they can talk about Ron's dilemma.

Jerome is April's least favorite of Ron's friends. Almost every time Ron and Jerome get together, Ron ends up in jail, the ER or passed out somewhere. April can't understand why Ron continues to make the same bad choices over and over again. He drinks like a fish when he's mad or stressed out even though his doctor told him to lay off the liquor and he gets with Jerome even though he knows it won't turn out well.

Ron has several level-headed friends he can call, but it never fails that he calls Jerome and ends up in a world of trouble. April is finally realizing that it's not Jerome that's the problem. Ron needs to make better decisions. April's steaming at the house and she's tired of putting up with Ron's excuses. Smooth talk and a make-up kiss tomorrow won't work this time.

Ron is a Punk that seeks solutions in all the wrong places!

We all know the definition of insanity; doing the same thing over and over and expecting a different result. Ron's a punk that continues to seek solutions in all the wrong people, places and things, expecting something he'll never get. Where do you go when you need answers? Who do you call? How do you self-medicate? The wise thing to do is to first mark off all the things that you've tried in the past that haven't worked and stop going in those directions. Your ex that wants you back probably isn't the person to confide in. The club or hang out that only temporarily makes you feel better isn't the spot either. Those pills, that liquor, that weed…no, those just drown out the pain for a minute, then what? Your bitter mother or depressed father probably won't offer the best advice either.

Seek wise counsel from an unbiased source; a mentor, a pastor, a healthy stable person. The Bible is a great source, inspired by the only person who knows you inside and out. Look for ways to apply its timeless wisdom. It doesn't matter how much you know if you're not willing to apply it. When I'm lost and looking for answers, I ask the Holy Spirit to reveal to me what seems to be hidden. It never fails to work when my patience doesn't get the best of me. That's usually half the problem, wanting what I want when I want it and not a second later. That's probably your problem too. We think, "If things don't work out when I want them to, I'll manufacture a solution for myself." Then you sit there wondering why things go from bad to worse.

If you are the punk that continues going in circles like a dog chasing his tail, STOP IT! You look ridiculous and you're only digging a deeper hole for yourself. The solution is only a prayer away. Sometimes we don't want to hear what's being revealed because it's not comfortable and it's contrary to our nature. Chances are, just stepping out on faith in a different direction will place you in the best position imaginable. Give it a try and stop seeking solutions in all the wrong places.

Punks Refuse to Adjust Unrealistic Expectations

"Oh me. Oh my." Yes, that's Brad's theme song. Brad is one miserable man. He wants his trophy wife to reappear and meet his needs and that's highly unlikely to happen. See, Brad's wife, Lorna, was diagnosed with a rare bone disease several years ago that has caused deformities in her spine. Lorna has come to grips with her limitations, but Brad refuses to face reality. He gets angry when Lorna isn't able to perform to his standards around the house and especially in the bedroom.

The doctors say Lorna is lucky because she is able to do many things that others with her disease can only dream about doing, but Brad doesn't see it that way. He has a picture in his mind of the perfect wife and ideal life and refuses to let it go to appreciate what he does have. Brad expects Lorna to live up to his expectations and has no problem letting her know that she's missing the mark.

Brad's treatment of Lorna breaks her parents' hearts. They have tried to convince Lorna to move back home with them. Lorna refuses stating that she loves Brad and he'll come around eventually. Today is Brad and Lorna's 12th wedding anniversary, which should be a happy occasion. Lorna is all dolled up looking forward to going out with Brad for a change, but Brad has no plans of coming home until long after Lorna's gone to bed. Not only is Brad a jerk...

Brad is also a Punk that refuses to adjust his unrealistic expectations!

I once lived next to an elderly couple. She was 80 and he was 90. I would often hear her fuss at her husband about various tasks she wanted him to do in their yard. Not only did she want them done, but she wanted them done a certain way. I reminded her, on an occasion or two, that her husband was 90 years old, not a spring chicken and besides their yard looked better than every yard on our block. It put us young bucks to shame. But because she never adjusted her unrealistic expectations, my neighbor was less content than she could have been. I'm just happy that her husband's hearing was poor, so he didn't hear all of her tirades.

Are your expectations of your spouse unrealistic like my neighbor's, yet you refuse to adjust them? How is that working for you? I know you're saying, "I have standards." Well, that's great, but unrealistic expectations will only leave you upset. If she is a size 14, but you expect her to be a size 2, it's probably not going to happen, at least not in a healthy way. Through sickness or stressing, maybe, but her frame may not be designed to be a size 2. If he's making $45,000 a year and you're expecting him to wine and dine you daily and shower you with extravagant gifts and get-aways, nope that's not realistic. On a six figure income maybe, but $45,000 a year is only enough to pay for the necessities and some occasional splurging. Now, he can go stick up a bank or sell some dope to give you what you want, but your wants aren't worth his life or his freedom.

    I'll admit, I'm a little disorganized. Ok, well, I'm a lot disorganized. So, for my husband to expect me to be neat and organized is unrealistic. It'll probably never happen. I can be more organized, but I'll never have my stuff lined up military style like his. On the other hand, my husband isn't the sentimental, mushy type. He will never sit and watch hours of chick flicks just for the fun of it, like me. We can enjoy one or two movies together, but three is pushing it. It is unrealistic for me to expect him to enjoy what I enjoy to the degree that I enjoy it. An adjustment of expectations decreases your stress level and frustration. It can make all the difference in the world in your marriage.

Punks Make Excuses Instead of Making Changes

Ann has an excuse for all of her issues. Her temper comes from having an Italian blood line. Her inability to budget her money is due to being overindulged by her father. She procrastinates because she's watched her mother do it for years and she can't be any other way. It's not Ann's fault that she's messy. She had a housekeeper when she was coming up and didn't have to clean up after herself.

Ann's husband, Wendell, has had all of these excuses thrown at him many times when he's tried to discuss Ann's issues and how they impact their family. Wendell doesn't want to hear another excuse. He wants to see some changes take place. Wendell's gone so far as to see a therapist to work on his shortcomings. Ann has even mentioned how she has noticed some positive changes, but Ann refuses to seek help. She says, "My family made me this way. This is how I am. I can't do anything about it."

Wendell is fed up. He just got the mortgage statement and Ann hasn't made a payment in two months. She agreed to do a *better job keeping up with the bills after the last fiasco, but obviously Ann hadn't kept up her end of the bargain. Wendell can't wait until Ann gets home to find out what excuse she has now and to hear where in the world the $1,800 went that should have gone to the mortgage company.*

Ann is a Punk that makes excuses instead of making changes!

"My mother made me this way." "I can't help it. My father taught me to be this way." "Nobody taught me to do that." If you spent as much time working on your character flaws as you did making excuses you'd be a new person by now. You know you need to change, but you continue to dwell on the reasons why you're so messed up instead of fixing your issues. You got this issue from your mother, that one from your father. They're the reason why you're full of defects. You don't understand why people can't see that and just leave you alone. You can't help it. You got this issue from your neighborhood and that one from being bullied as a kid. Your ex-boyfriend is the cause of that issue.

No doubt, we've all been negatively affected by the people in our lives in one way or another, whether you were abused, neglected, overly pampered, talked about, manipulated, lied to or whatever. But at some point you have to take responsibility for your healing, for yourself and move from victim to overcomer. No, it's not easy, but it's necessary if you want to grow. You are not the only person whose mother didn't want them. You are not the only person who was told that you wouldn't amount to anything. You are not the only person who was wrongly accused.

Don't remain a punk who makes excuses instead of making changes. How many people came to your pity party last year? How about last month? What about yesterday? Chances are, you sent out a lot of invitations, but nobody showed up. Marriage can be an awesome thing, but not when you're married to a punk who refuses to do what's necessary to become a healthy happy individual. Marriage to a punk who continually makes excuses instead of making changes, takes a lot of energy and work. When you don't hold up your end, your mate has to assume responsibility for your part and theirs. You may be saying,

"I'd do it for him/her if the shoe was on the other foot." Well, we'll never know will we because you'll be making excuses about your excuses before you know it.

Punks Don't Take the Time to Get to Know Themselves

If you ask Gale to tell you about herself, she'll no doubt tell you about the last 5 people she's dated. You see, Gale is never alone long enough to get to know who she is outside of a relationship. When she was seeing Steve the pilot, she was an adventurous world-traveler. When she was with Milton the missionary, she was a humanitarian. When she was in love with Jason the drummer, she was a music enthusiast.

Gale has no clue who she truly is. She doesn't know what she is passionate about or what drives her, besides men. Gale just hitches her wagon to her latest beau's stallion and she's off and running. The problem is that Gale is unable to bring much value to her relationships because she doesn't even know the value that is inside of her. Gale sucks her relationships dry and doesn't understand why they all end up the same way.

Gale is brokenhearted once again. Her latest relationship with Lance the architect just ended. It was a rebound from her relationship with Clarence the teacher, so she's really not sure which relationship she's grieving. Her friends keep trying to convince her to slow down and take some time for herself, but she has no intentions of doing that.

Gale is a Punk that hasn't taken the time to get to know herself!

Who are you? What is your purpose in life? What are you passionate about? What are your deepest fears? What makes you unique? The worst thing a person can do is marry someone before they know the answer to these questions. For the punk who marries before knowing these answers, the answers depend on who they are with at the time or who they believe others want them to be. Punks don't take the time to get to know who they are. They are like chameleons, changing to fit their surroundings. They eventually lose sight of themselves totally. It's a shame because we are all uniquely made with gifts and talents, like no one else.

There is a place in this world that only you can fill by being who God created you to be. When that doesn't happen, there's a big hole. Now punk, you wouldn't want someone to fall through that hole because you're not being true to yourself would you? If you've never been without a relationship you may fall in this category.

Ever since you had your first kiss in the kindergarten coat closet you've been sprung. No wonder you don't know whether you're coming or going. Take some time to get to know what makes you tick. Don't let others define who you are or who you should be. Psalm 139:14 says you are fearfully and wonderfully made. It just may take some digging to get to the core of who you are.

If you are constantly stressing to be everything to everyone, you're the punk I'm talking about. You don't have time to do the things that God has for you because you're too busy running around doing everything else. How can you be the husband or wife that complements your spouse when you're all over the place? You're a counterfeit trying to pass, but it won't work. Figure out who you are first for yourself and then you can take your rightful place in marriage and in life.

Punks are Stuck in the Past

Juan can't enjoy today because he's too consumed with what happened yesterday. Spend 10 minutes with Juan and you will quickly know 2 things; about his basketball career that crashed due to an ankle injury and about his past relationship that ended just as tragically. The failure of his past relationship always seems to be in the forefront of his mind. "If only she had done X, we would still be together." "If only I had done Y, we could have made it work." What Juan doesn't realize is that his dwelling on the past isn't setting him up for a good relationship in the future. His dwelling actually has him stuck and what he is focusing on is growing rather than shrinking. Punk, no woman wants to hear you rehash your failed relationships.

Juan not only obsesses over past relationships, he also obsesses over his missed opportunities. Juan is an educated man. He has 2 successful businesses and a huge support network of family and friends. Juan has a lot going for himself, but he talks about his basketball career as if it is the only thing that he had going for himself. Juan's so stuck in the past that he can't appreciate his wonderful present or see the bright future ahead of him.

Juan is a Punk that's stuck in the past!

One surefire way to get into a car accident is to keep looking in the rear view mirror and not focus on what's in front of you. The same is true with our lives. Some punks are so focused on the past that they can't plan for the future. Their lives are an accident waiting to happen. What's back there anyway; the one that got away, failed relationships, errors in judgment, mistakes, missed opportunities, oh yeah, the good ole days?

If you think your best days are behind you, you might as well call the undertaker, order your casket, ask Sista Jenkins to sing your favorite song and lay out your burial clothes because you've stopped living. "You know I used to be something back in the day." Well, that's great to know because the person that you are now is not going anywhere and has stopped living.

Do you have mistakes that are eating you alive? Do you have regrets or remorse that you can't move past? If you need to, make amends and move on. You can't continue to punish yourself for the things in your past. Do you have great memories of the past? Good, make some more today. If you don't want your spouse to go on without you, don't stay stuck in the past. Grieve if you must, but don't stay there. Marriage isn't about your past. It's about creating a legacy, a future, experiencing life together.

Punks are so focused on the past that the present creeps right past them. Don't let your response to your mate's petition to try new things be, "I've already done that." If you haven't experienced it with your spouse, it couldn't have been the same. Or you should have at least warned your mate that you have been everywhere and done everything, so they would know not to bother you to try anything or go anywhere. Be kind to yourself and your spouse. Grant yourself permission to enjoy today, create new memories and even make a few mistakes along the way.

Punks Are Controlling

Lynn's world has somehow become very small. She was once close to her family, but now she rarely talks to them, let alone see them in person. Lynn can recall being popular and having many friends, but she can now count her friends on one hand and they're all ones that her husband, Cletus, approves of.

Early in her marriage, Lynn would talk to her family and friends on a regular basis, despite Cletus' objections. She just ignored his probing and negativity. Over the years, she's grown tired of hearing Cletus' mouth and just resigned to seeing her family and friends when she could.

Cletus also controls practically every other area of Lynn's life from what she wears, to her hobbies, even her choice of careers. Lynn's not sure when she handed her life over to Cletus. What was once a little annoying is beyond ridiculous now. Since Cletus lost his "good" job at the foundry, his controlling ways have only continued to get worse.

Lynn's 20 year reunion is quickly approaching, but she's afraid to even mention it to Cletus. She'd love to reconnect with some of her old friends, but Cletus' controlling ways would definitely put a damper on the occasion!

Cletus is a controlling Punk!

"Where are you going?" "Who are you going with?" "Who's going to be there?" "You can't go if I don't go." "Dress this way." "Walk this way." "Talk this way." Some people don't need spouses, they need children. Well, that wouldn't work either because children grow up and eventually begin to make their own decisions. Punks, don't like that. They love control.

Why does one grown person need another grown person to control their every move? They don't. So punk, stop being controlling of your mate. He doesn't need you to map out his life. She doesn't need you to tell her what to do and when to do it. It takes a very insecure person to think that they need to control someone else. Are you scared that she'll leave you if you give her room to breathe? She may. Do you think he'll realize his brain works just fine and he doesn't need you if he has a chance to think for himself? He probably would.

Do you feel powerless in all other areas, so this is your way of feeling strong and powerful? That's not your mate's fault. Go get some help! Have you placed yourself on a throne and think it's your job to tell your man/woman what to do because you know what's right and wrong and they don't? You're not nearly as smart as you think you are if that's the way you think. God allows us to choose and He is *actually* sitting on a throne.

You may need to be alone for a little while so you can appreciate your spouse. Your mate deserves to be happy and your controlling ways don't make anyone happy except you. If you desire a great relationship, try something different. Stop exerting your control over your mate and practice some self-control.

Punks Can't Hold Water

Quinten can't hold water. For those who have never heard this phrase, it means he tells everything that he is told. This idiosyncracy has proven to be detrimental to many people close to Quinten, including his fiancé, Trina.

Trina confided in Quinten one day that she wasn't sure if her youngest brother was her father's child. She told Quinten that she had overheard her mother talking on the phone to a friend trying to figure out how to break this news to her husband, Trina's father. Since overhearing her mom's conversation, this had been weighing heavy on Trina's mind. Trina said it felt good to talk to Quinten about the situation and she asked that Quinten keep it to himself because it could ruin her family if the secret got out.

While at work a few weeks later, talking to a co-worker about "dysfunctional" families, Quinten told his co-worker about the "paternity" issue in Trina's family. Unbeknownst to Quinten, the co-worker's mother was an acquaintance of Trina's father. You can imagine what happened next.

Quinten couldn't understand why Trina was so irate when she heard what Quinten had done. After talking to Quinten's sister, Trina realized that no one shares information with Quinten that they don't want shared with the world. Well, that's great to know moving forward, but now Trina's in the middle of her mama and daddy's drama and it doesn't feel too good.

Quinten is a Punk That Can't Hold Water!

Do you think it is ok to divulge the information that your spouse shares with you in confidence? Do you share things with others about your spouse that you know your spouse would prefer that you keep to yourself; his idiosyncrasies or flaws? Punk, keep your mouth shut. You don't want others knowing your private business, so why do you share your mate's personal information so easily?

"I tell my mama everything. We're best friends." Well, that may have worked yesterday, but, today you and your mama need different boundaries in your relationship. Your mama needs to get a life and stay out of yours and you need to do likewise. She doesn't need to know your husband's business and besides why would she want to?

Marriage involves intimacy and vulnerability. Your spouse should be able to talk to you in confidence and know that the conversation will go no further. If you are a talkative spouse who shares the nuances of your relationship and breaks your spouse's confidence by telling their business to the world, you are a destructive force to your marriage. Get a journal. Share to your heart's content and get it off your chest, but don't expose your spouse.

And stop putting all of your business on social media. You don't have to mention names in order for everyone to know who you're talking about. If you can't keep it to yourself find a good therapist. At least that way you can get some sound advice and solutions.

It's your job to cover your spouse's weaknesses not to feed him/her to the wolves. That does not mean that you ignore their wrongful actions. You confront them in love. But if your spouse can't share their innermost thoughts with you, a huge gaping hole will be present in your marriage. And ol' girl and ol' boy would love to lend an ear.

No one needs to know how well your mate does or doesn't perform in the bedroom. It's no one's business other than the two of you and God, oh, and maybe a sex therapist. You can either thank God for your spouse's sexual strengths or pray and ask for some help in that area, either way, He definitely should be a part of your intimate life. Now, your mother on the other hand and your boys or your girls, it's none of their business. Punk, keep that information to yourself. Your spouse's business is not to be shared with the world.

Use wisdom and just ask yourself "is this something that is ok to share or something that I need to keep to myself?" When in doubt, shut your mouth. Sounds kind of catchy doesn't it? Commit it to memory because it will come in handy time and time again in marriage. And just because he/she didn't say to keep it to yourself does not give you the right to share it. Ask yourself, "Why am I sharing this information"? Do you want someone to take your side on an issue? Do you want some attention or some sympathy? None of these are good reasons to let others into your relationship. If you know it will hurt your relationship or hurt your spouse, zip your lips.

Punks Fail to Leave and Cleave

Jill is really fed up with Ben. For the third time this month he has cancelled their "date night." Jill says she could understand if it was an emergency or something important that comes up, but Ben drops everything when his parents call to run simple errands. This time Ben even forgot to tell her that they weren't going to the art museum.

Jill thought it was cute how close Ben was to his parents, particularly his mother, when they first started going out. Although he was 37, he still lived at home, but this didn't raise a red flag to Jill because many families seemed to be sharing homes to cut back on living expenses.

Jill thought Ben was very respectful to ask his parents if it was ok for Jill to stop by when they dated. Jill had no idea what she was in for. Ben consults his parents on everything from where to vacation to what laundry detergent to purchase. Ben's parents' vote actually holds more weight than Jill's does.

Ben's parents call constantly and drop by regularly without calling. Jill was shocked to hear that Ben stops by his parents' home almost daily after work and has been for the past 4 years. No wonder he is seldom hungry when he gets home. Jill is a pretty descent cook so it can't be about her culinary skills.

Ben is a Punk that failed to leave and cleave!

When the Bible speaks about leaving and cleaving, it's not speaking about physically leaving the nest. In Biblical times, it was common for several generations to live under one roof. What leaving and cleaving refers to is an emotional umbilical cord. A cord that gets in the way of husband and wife "cleaving", connecting emotionally and spiritually. "My mama does it this way." "My daddy said this is the best." "My mother prefers this…" Punks refuse to leave and cleave. They may have physically left the nest, but mentally and emotionally they're still there. Many times this is done on such a subconscious level that they don't recognize the destructive undercurrent that's threatening their marriage.

Punks refuse to start their own traditions and carve out their own niche in life. Her husband can't be himself because he is constantly being compared to her father. His wife can't be herself because she is being compared to his mother. It won't be long before resentment and bitterness take root. No one wants a spouse who has to continuously consult their mama and daddy about everything. Yes, you should seek wise counsel, but your parents should not be in the middle of your marriage. God should be.

 A three strand cord is not easily broken. This is true if God is that third strand, but totally false if your mother or father is that third strand. Cut that apron string right now punk, before your wife bids you farewell. If your motto is WWMD (What Would Mama Do?) or WWDD (What would Daddy Do?) then you've probably failed to leave and cleave.

 When you say "I do" you join with another person to create a life, a home that works for the two of you. If you can't make a move without checking in with one of your parents, there is a problem. In marriage, the goal is not to recreate your parents' family, but to create a family of your own. Your parents' advice should not overrule your spouse's. They should not have a greater or equal say-so in your household decisions.

Of course you will use what was instilled in you by your parents to some degree or another, but that's just a starting point, other factors must also be taken into consideration, like your spouse.

Some people are never ready to leave home. That's ok, stay home with your mama and daddy, Princess, Lil' Man, but don't bring your parents into your marriage. Your spouse should not be in competition with your parents. He should not be constantly reminded about how great a man your father is/was, how wonderful he was at maintaining the home. She should not be constantly told how great a woman your mother is/was, how well she cooks and sewed your socks. Punk, if it was that great, why did you leave? I'm just saying. Give your spouse an opportunity to do things his/her way. When you visit your parents that's when you can get it their way.

Punks Refuse to Say "I'm Sorry"

Marcus scraped his wife Carol's car on the garage door the day after she bought it. Ouch! Did Carol get a sincere apology? If you think she did, you don't know Marcus. What Carol got was excuses as to why the car got scraped and how it really wasn't Marcus' fault.

In the 14 years that Marcus and Carol have been married, Marcus has never apologized for anything. When he accidentally shut Carol's finger in the door, NOPE. When he accused Carol of losing his pocket watch, which he had hidden from himself, NOPE. When he forgot to tell Carol that one of her most important clients had called, NOPE. When he ate the cookies that Carol had made for a work pitch-in, NOPE.

Marcus thinks apologizing is for punks, but what he doesn't realize is that it takes a real man to own up to his mistakes and apologize. The sad part is that Marcus expects to be apologized to when he is offended. Poor Marcus needs to be taught the Golden Rule, to do unto others as you would have them to do unto you. I'm not sure if Marcus is just stubborn or a little slow, but he has no idea how much he has hurt his marriage and his wife.

Marcus is a Punk that refuses to say, "I'm sorry"!

Spend enough time with anyone and eventually you're going to say or do something that warrants an apology. If you can't say "I'm sorry" you're a punk who needs to work that out before saying "I do". The road to divorce is paved with unacknowledged offenses, big and small. Pride causes us to refuse to accept and make amends for our faults.

There is no better place to practice crucifying flesh and disposing of pride than in marriage. "Sorry for the hurtful words I spoke" "Sorry for my lack of consideration" "Sorry for neglecting you". That can all take place in one day. Imagine what 10 years of marital conversation could look like. But the goal is not to continue to commit offenses.

The goal is to strive to be a better person daily and when you fall short to acknowledge your shortcomings, make amends ("what can I do to right this wrong") and to move forward. If you are human, you will make mistakes. There is no way around it. Saying you're sorry acknowledges the offense and lets the offended person know that you have remorse for what you've said or done.

Maybe you don't say you're sorry because you don't believe you've done anything wrong or maybe you believe your spouse deserves to be treated or talked to in an offensive way. Whatever the case, you need to ask God to soften your hardened heart and mold you into being, first of all, a kind hearted person and then a good spouse. Psychopaths have no remorse. Is that what you are, punk? Is your heart and mind so clouded with pain that you no longer care about afflicting pain on others? Have you placed yourself on a pedestal and refuse to show "weakness" by acknowledging your shortcomings and wrongful deeds?

Your actions should back up your words. If you're sorry for gambling away the bill money, you can show that you're sorry by doing the right thing rather than repeating the same offensive act. You may need to hand over your check to your more responsible mate while you get some help for your gambling problem. Don't let your pride stand in the way of your healing.

Punks are Pushovers

Do you need $500 to get out of a bind, a last minute baby sitter, someone to drop their plans at the drop of a dime to help you out? Call Nellie, she's that girl. Keith thought Nellie was just a thoughtful person when they started going out. Her friend's would call her needing this or that and Nellie would promptly accommodate their requests.

Nellie co-signed for a car for her sister and got stuck with the note when her sister refused to pay. Due to this financial burden, Nellie was unable to get a new car for herself when her transmission went out. Nellie refused to confront her sister or even mention the strain that her sister's irresponsibility had put on her.

Nellie's brother came for a visit 9 months ago. He never left. Nellie continues to send hints that she wants him to leave, but she refuses to directly address the situation. Her brother has taken over her 2 bedroom condo. She can no longer park her car in her garage because his belongings are stacked up from wall to wall.

Keith and Nellie have been dating for 2 ½ years and he has witnessed Nellie being taken advantage of on more occasions than he cares to remember. When he brings it to Nellie's attention and tells her that she is teaching people how to treat her, she says it's no big deal.

Keith wants to propose but knows that he can't take on the burden of Nellie's soft ways. If they marry, not only will these users be taking advantage of Nellie, but they will be taking advantage of him too. Keith knows that he would never put up with that treatment.

Nellie is a pushover Punk!

You get punked out of everything, from your hard earned cash to your time to your peace of mind. You may see yourself as being super loving and exceptionally giving, but your inability to set healthy boundaries is a sign that something is seriously wrong. You are a punk of epic proportions and the sharks smell blood. What are you afraid of: conflict, being alone, being exposed? Are you too afraid to stand up for yourself? Are you motivated by guilt? Do you need to feel needed? Whatever it is, deal with it.

Once you stop allowing others' dreams, desires, and needs to consume you, you'll have an opportunity to focus on what God wants you to do and who He wants you to become.

In a marriage saying, "Yes" too much is just as destructive as saying, "No" too much. How can your spouse learn, grow and mature if you're doing, being and thinking for them? Stop it!

I can attest. I was once that pushover, people pleaser. It seems like it's been decades ago now. *Whew.* I can breathe and decide what is mine to take on and what is not.

I always thought it was strange to hear a woman say that a man was *too* nice. First thing I would think was, "She just wants a thug" or "She's just looking for someone to beat on her." That's not necessarily true. It's close to impossible to be in a healthy relationship with a person who doesn't have a backbone. Just as a child needs boundaries and limits to be set, adults also need to set boundaries for one another.

If you are a pushover, your "niceness" will negatively impact your spouse. You won't have the time or energy to handle your own responsibilities which will, no doubt, affect your relationship with your spouse. Do you expect your spouse to sit back and watch you being walked on and used? A loving spouse would be infuriated. Besides, you're crippling the folks that you think you're helping. (Thanks Honey for loving me enough to tell me the truth).

It's hard to transform from punk pushover to assertive and balanced, but once you make the transition you'll be lighter and much more free. Your mind and your pockets will thank you. There's no better day than today, to grow a backbone and to set some boundaries.

Punks Have No Sense of Humor

When Kris met Dan, she was drawn to his serious demeanor. She knew he was much different than the guys that she had attracted in the past. "I'm sure this brother takes care of business" is what she thought. Dan was the oldest of 4 kids and often put in charge to look after his siblings when his mother worked or attended classes. He barely had time to play with kids his age because he had to keep the house in order and make sure his school work was completed.

It took a few months for Kris to notice that Dan rarely laughed, even when they watched comedies or hung out with her silly friends. He was always serious and refused to let his guard down and have fun. Kris would sometimes hold back her laughter when she was around Dan because he had a way of making her feel immature or like a slacker.

The final straw was when Dan stormed out of the room after sitting on a whoopee cushion that Kris' 6 year old niece had placed in his chair. Everyone in the room busted out in laughter, other than Dan. He said he felt humiliated and couldn't believe that Kris was laughing too. Kris told Dan that he needed to lighten up. She also told him that they both needed to cut their losses. She couldn't see herself with someone who couldn't enjoy a good laugh.

Dan is a Punk with no sense of humor!

What is life without laughter? I don't know, but I hope I never have to find out. Humor is important in our lives and especially in our marriages. It's a gift from God. It brings an extra something, something to the mundane. Laughter is good for the mind, the body and the soul. It can diffuse an explosive situation and take the edge off during a stressful moment. And if you can't laugh at yourself, you're in trouble. Whether it is something you thought, said or did, there is plenty to laugh at in the course of a day. Punk, don't take yourself or life too serious.

Yes, there are times to be reserved and serious, but there are more times to laugh and be silly. Why are you so uptight? What would happen if you giggled, chuckled or had one of those deep down gut laughs? Your body would relax and you would feel better. You would be better prepared to deal with life's stresses. The worse thing that people lacking a sense of humor do is they don't want other people to enjoy laughter either, "What's so funny?" "That's not funny." "You're silly." Stop being uptight and start enjoying the funny aspects of life. You don't have to laugh at everything, like I do, but you should laugh at least 5 times a day. Don't ask where that number came from because it just sounded like a good number. 10 sounds even better.

If you burp during a corporate speech, that's messed up, but find the humor in it and move on. I know some things are inappropriate to laugh at, but every situation that you can find humor in, do. You'll start to not only feel better, but you'll look better too. The muscles in your face will relax and the people around you will relax.

Marriage can be trying and difficult, but laughter sprinkled throughout can lessen the pain during those times and make them more bearable. If you and your honey don't have your own inside jokes, get some. These are things that are funny to the two of you that means nothing to other people. This forms a connection, a bond in your marriage. The two of you are on the inside and the rest of the world is on the outside.

And when you laugh so hard you tinkle a little bit or let one slip out, that's when you know you've had a good laugh. Punk, I know you've got your nose turned up, but don't knock it til you've tried it.

Punks Stop Studying Their Spouse

Althea and Max have been married for 8 years. Both agree that the first 5 years were amazing. They were both building their careers, but they were intentional when it came to spending time together and meeting each other's needs.

Althea is still on cloud nine but Max is sorely disappointed. You see, Max still lavishes Althea with the things that make her soul sing while Althea has grown complacent. It is evident that Althea has stopped studying Max. He has changed over the years, but she hasn't taken notice. Max tries to share his new passions and aspects of himself with Althea, but she disregards the new information and reverts back to the old information.

Max enjoys using new discoveries about Althea to pleasantly surprise her from time to time, but he can't understand why Althea still buys him golf paraphernalia although he stopped playing 3 years ago after tearing his rotary cuff. Now, what Max does enjoy now is mentoring teen boys at the recreation center. He's been doing it for over 2 years and is always looking for ways to build deeper relationships with his mentees.

Althea is in her own little world oblivious to what brings a smile to her man's face.

Althea is the Punk who has stopped studying her man!

In many professions, in order to maintain a license, an individual must complete a certain number of Continuing Education Units otherwise known as CEU's on a set basis. Some people who need CEU's are: teachers, mental health professionals, social workers, architects, engineers and pest control operators. These individuals continue to study their craft knowing that should they falter their license goes "bye-bye". A marriage is much more important than being a pest control operator or even a social worker, but punks don't invest the necessary time and effort to accumulate marital CEU's.

How many CEU's have you accumulated during your marriage? The reason that CEU's are required in the fields mentioned above and many others is to ensure that our knowledge and skills are up to date. If an architect received his degree 30 years ago and never pursued continued learning, he'd be lost today. So much has changed. If you don't continue to study your man or your woman, his likes, her dislikes, you're killing your marriage. She's not the same woman that she was 5 years ago. Hopefully she's grown and matured. He's not the same man that he was last year. Prayerfully he's a better him.

Punk if you think that acquiring marital CEU's is too time-consuming then you're not ready to get your marriage license. Becoming a mental health professional is hard work. Anyone who goes through the long hours of studying and sacrificing to get that license will not give it up so quickly. It cost them something. The most important license that you may ever get is on the line. Don't be nonchalant and lazy.

Are you ok with a bachelor's degree? How about a high school diploma? No, you barely got your GED in knowing your mate and you're fine with that. Your spouse is worthy of post graduate work, so stop skipping classes, punk, and put some real effort into knowing this person that you've committed your life to. What does he like? What doesn't she like? What does he fear? What makes her giddy like a little girl? What turns him off? What turns her on?

What grade would your spouse give you in regards to your current knowledge of him/her? Would it be an "A" for your acute eye for detail or an "F" for extreme neglect? Do you need to request some extra credit to get up to par? I personally don't mind staying after class. I guess I'm a nerd, but I'd rather be a nerd than a dropout.

I hate to break it to you, but there's someone who would love to study the course that you keep skipping out on and neglecting. You got a scholarship and you're taking it for granted. They're willing to take out a student loan to finance what they deem to be valuable.

Go ahead, pull out your notebook and a pen. Start taking notes. And don't stop next year or 10 years from now. Keep coming back for your CEUs. Excel in knowing your mate. Your Honors Diploma awaits you.

Punks Expect Perfection

"He dresses too loud." "I don't like short men." "He doesn't earn enough." Liz has met several great men, but none of them meet her standards. They're not perfect. They love the Lord, they have no fatal flaws and they're respectful and responsible, but she won't give them the time of day.

Liz dissects men and finds an issue with them before they have a chance. There was Kenny, he cared for his sick mother which made him a "mama's boy" in Liz's eyes. She was too short-sighted to see that Kenny would take care of her too one day if the need arose. Then there was Sam. He had a slight limp due to a motorcycle accident. Liz couldn't imagine walking down the aisle with him. Then there was Johnny. He had an overbite or was it an underbite? Whatever the case, Liz couldn't see past his dental imperfections. She thought to herself, "I can't take a chance of my children having jacked up grills. That'll cost a fortune." Liz has turned down more offers to dinner than you would imagine. She's holding out for Mr. Perfect. Liz is in for a rude awakening. She won't find Mr. Perfect here on earth.

Liz is a Punk that expects perfection!

What one person sees as perfect and what another person sees as perfection are miles apart. What images of the perfect spouse have you conjured up in your mind? Does she iron your clothes meticulously? Does he excel in a certain industry? Does he cook like a chef du jour? Does she look like a run-way model? Only you know what that idea of perfection is in your mind that you're expecting from your mate.

Punk, you're setting yourself up for great disappointment because, besides God, there truly is nothing constant, but change. Her looks will change. All the liposuction, plastic surgeries, exercising, and injections can't ward it off forever. His looks will change too. The six pack may one day become a keg, and he may shave his head to spare himself the embarrassment of cow licks or a receding hairline. His profession may change, her abilities will change, his likes/dislikes will change. Then what? What will you do when they no longer fit in your perfect box? Replace them or sulk? Well, guess what? You'll change too. It can all happen so quickly and you'll want someone in your corner who can embrace you in all your imperfection. Actually, in your best state you aren't perfect either so why do you hold someone to your idea of perfection.

So, she's no longer a size 6. Dude, she had four of your kids. Get over it. On the other hand, ladies that doesn't mean that you should let yourself go and stop working out and eating right. If you've gained 100 pounds over the course of your relationship, he probably is like "dang, what happened to my banging babe?" The same goes for you guys. Once you get her, that's not the time to let your six pack transform into a keg. Ladies like to have someone who resembles the person that they fell in love with too. If you've changed due to issues beyond your control, it's acceptance time for you and your mate. Address areas that are in your control and ask God to help you to let the rest go. Work on being grateful for the gift of life and all the great blessings that come with it.

Real people have real ups and downs. Does the perfect person never get angry, never complain, never make requests, never feel depressed? Sorry, but humans have a range of emotions and we can experience many of them in the same day, sometimes the same hour. Perfect? What does that look like to you? Believe it or not, you're not perfect. So, don't expect someone else to be something that you're not. You get that, punk? Snap out of it!

I'm Still Not Sold on this Punk Thing

You may be wondering what's the big deal? Or saying to yourself, 'Yes, I have a few issues just like everybody else. Who are you to call me a punk and call me out on my stuff?' Look, you can continue doing what you've been doing and no doubt you will continue to get the same results that you've been getting. If that works for you then, ok, but if you want a different result and a different experience then you're going to have to do some things differently and it starts with looking at and addressing YOUR mess.

Ask yourself how is my spouse or significant other effected by...my controlling ways, my single's mentality, my inability to hold water... or how will my future spouse/marriage be effected if I don't address my mess. Remember, a punk is a person who refuses to address their relationship-repellent attitudes, behaviors, and characteristics. If your mate likes or doesn't mind a part of you that's been described as "punk ways" or is turned on by it then this isn't a relationship-repellent attitude, behavior or characteristic as far as your relationship is concerned. I've used examples of what will cause many relationships to erode if not addressed.

Take some time to look back over the stories and my flawed attempt to describe what these attitudes, behaviors, and characteristics look like and be honest with yourself. Ask those who are close to you and know you well to give you some feedback on what they see in you that you may not see in yourself (your blind spots) and don't get mad when they tell you the truth.

If the scenario has minor details that are different than the way that you operate, don't get caught up in those details and use them as an excuse to deny the bigger picture of what does fit you and most importantly what's going to stand between you and your chance of a healthy happy union.

The section below will give you an opportunity to pull it all together and inventory yourself. This part can be given to your spouse, a close friend, or someone else who knows you well. Use it to get one step closer to annihilating the punk and moving toward growth, healing, and wholeness.

Inventory

In this section, check the attitudes, behaviors and characteristics that resonate with you. You may see these tendencies in yourself or you may have been told a time or two that someone else sees these things in you (which doesn't make it true, but can offer you some insight). If you're not married, answer in terms of your tendencies in previous relationships (if applicable), "if I was married", "when I marry" or "when I was married previously".

If you check an attitude, behavior or characteristic as one that feels true to you, put a brief statement of why you checked it to be true. If you do not check it you're not off the hook. Put a brief statement of why it doesn't apply to you on the lines provided. The corresponding explanations should also be completed by the person(s) that are completing the inventory on your behalf. Take a deep breath…now move forward courageously!

Check those that resonate with you (this is a good time to refer back to what you've read thus far)

○ Marry for All the Wrong Reasons

_____
_____
_____
_____

○ Don't Want to Work

_____
_____
_____
_____

○ Send Their Representative

_____
_____
_____
_____

○ Continue to Act Single After Saying "I Do"

_____
_____
_____

_____
_____

O Exploit Vulnerabilities
_____
_____
_____
_____

O Walk into Marriage with an Out in Mind
_____
_____
_____
_____

O Think They Know-It-All
_____
_____
_____
_____

○ Run When Things Get Tough

_____
_____
_____
_____
_____

○ Seek Solutions in All the Wrong Places

_____
_____
_____
_____
_____

○ Refuse to Adjust Unrealistic Expectations

_____
_____
_____
_____
_____

○ Make Excuses Instead of Making Changes

_____
_____

_____
_____
_____

O Don't Take the Time to Get to Know Themselves

_____
_____
_____
_____

O Are Stuck in the Past

_____
_____
_____
_____

O Are Controlling

_____
_____
_____
_____

○ Can't Hold Water

_____
_____
_____
_____

○ Fail to Leave and Cleave

_____
_____
_____
_____

○ Refuse to Say "I'm Sorry"

_____
_____
_____
_____

○ Are Pushovers

_____
_____
_____
_____

○ Have No Sense of Humor

_____
_____
_____
_____

○ Stop Studying Their Spouse

_____
_____
_____
_____

○ Expect Perfection

_____
_____
_____
_____

You are Undeniably a Punk. Now What?

I've made light of some serious issues that we face as humans. I've called everyone a punk from the man that refused to work to the woman who expected perfection. In all seriousness, these issues aren't the real issue. The issue is when you have issues and refuse to address them. That's what makes a punk a punk. It's the refusal to address the relationship-repellent attitude, behavior or characteristic that stands in the way of the great marriage that you could have. It's the refusal to change, to grow, to become a better you.

You want a great marriage, but you're a punk. Now what? You have two choices. You can either attack your mess head on or you can ignore it at the expense of your relationship. Only you can make the choice to change.

Denial is your worst enemy when it comes to your mess. Your relationship-repellent attitudes, behaviors and characteristics have probably been a part of you for so long that you've grown accustomed to them or minimized their impact on your life. You may even believe that your issues will just work themselves out. Don't fool yourself. Your mess won't go away without some work on your part. The longer you wait to address it, the worse it is going to get.

Everyone has issues. Some are big and some are small. Some are life impacting and some are so miniscule that they go unnoticed. We all have mess to deal with. That's just a part of being human, but there is also a process that we must go through to get to the other side. I call this process Triple A: Acknowledge, Address and Accountability.

First, you need to acknowledge your issues. Be honest with yourself. What are your shortcomings? In what ways are you a punk? As you read this book, which chapters made you say, "That sounds like me?" What changes do you need to make to become a great partner? This would be a great time to ask for honest input from those close to you. Ask God to show you the areas that you need to deal with. He will take your blinders off and allow you to see yourself, maybe for the first time.

Then, you must address your mess. Begin by asking God to help you to change. Don't fool yourself by thinking that you can handle it on your own. If you could make the changes on your own, wouldn't you have done so by now? God can transform you and He can also provide you with resources to address your mess. You may need to see a therapist or seek counsel from your pastor or spiritual advisor. This is the work phase. It won't be easy and you will probably want to give up, but don't short-change yourself. Engage in the process and watch what will unfold.

Alright, now you need to find someone who can hold you accountable. This is someone who will call you on your mess and not take your lame excuses. This person needs to be accessible and someone that you can respect. Your accountability partner will be trusted with intimate details about you so don't take this person's role lightly.

Annihilating your inner punk will change the course of your life and enrich your relationships. It will also positively impact your community. You will become the man/woman that God called you to be and the by-product will be your ability to be a great spouse. Once you've put in the work, get ready to say "farewell" to the punk and "hello" to the new you! I pray that you grow to more intimately know yourself and Jesus on your journey.

www.ingramcontent.com/pod-product-compliance
Lightning Source LLC
Chambersburg PA
CBHW061450040426
42450CB00007B/1304